BookRags Literature Study Guide

Freak the Mighty by Rodman Philbrick

Copyright Information

ISBN: 978-1-304-48936-4

Table of Contents

Plot Summary

The story of "Freak the Mighty" begins with Max looking back on his friendship with Kevin, or as Max affectionately refers to him as, Freak. Max first encounters Freak when they are both in pre-school. He recalls Freak bursting into the nursery school like he owns the place. His head is normal sized but his body is small and twisted beneath him. Freak has shiny silver braces on his legs and proclaims loudly to everyone that he is a robot. Max has his own problems, he is unusually large and a little on the rough side, in fact, there are those, including his loving grandparents, who think he is downright violent--or fears he will be someday. Freak does not last long at the pre-school and Max does not see him again until the third grade when he just catches a glimpse of him on the short bus.

The summer before eighth grade, to Max's surprise, Freak and his mom, the beautiful Gwen, move just a few doors away from him. Max is too shy to talk to Freak but he watches him from behind some bushes. Freak spots Max and tells the "earthling" to show himself, which is the beginning of their unusual friendship. Max has never known anyone as smart as Freak--he can speak on any subject. His vocabulary is also impressive. Max has to ask him continually what he is talking about or stay silent and pretend he knows. Freak is equally impressed with Max--he is so big and strong. Nobody messes with this guy.

At a 4th of July fireworks celebration, Freak cannot see the display due of his small stature. Max, without asking, lifts Freak's light body up on his wide strong shoulders. Freak is not offended--on the contrary he is delighted. He sees the show and for the first time in his life feels taller than everyone. On that night, "Freak the Mighty" is born. For the next year, it is not an unusual sight to see Max walking along with Kevin perched on his shoulders. They complete each other. Max is happy to finally have a brain on his soldiers and Freak is in heaven traversing the terrain on the longest legs he ever dreamed of.

The two boys become best friends who go on quests and adventures dreamed up by the brain--Kevin. The Freak fantasizes about being one of the Knights of the Round Table. In fact, he closely identifies with King Arthur, who as a young, weak boy is the only one in Camelot who can pull the magical sword Excalibur out of its stone. Kevin is determined to slay all the dragons and monsters out there. Perched atop of Max, he guides his steed--Max that is--to quest after quest. Unfortunately, one dragon they cannot slay is the one that is taking place inside Max's body. His organs are growing faster than his crippled body.

The two boys are able to defeat a very bad monster; when together they are able to elude Max's father, Killer Ken, who has kidnapped Max and is ready to kill him. The memories rush back to Max of when he is four years old and witnesses his father killing his mother. After Freak uses his water gun to shoot a stinging liquid into Ken's eyes, his rampage is soon over and he is back in police custody.

Freak does not make it past the first year mark of their friendship and the one year anniversary of "Freak the Mighty." Before he leaves, he insists that Max write the story of their adventures and quests. Max does not think he can do it, but is compelled to do so by the memory of his young friend who believed in him.

Chapters 1 and 2 Summary

Chapter 1: The Unvanquished Truth

Max begins his story by declaring that he did not have a brain until he connected with the Freak in the eighth grade. From a very young age, Max is raised by his grandparents. His mother is dead and his father is not on the scene. The grandparents have problems with the aggressiveness of Max and place him in a pre-school with kids his age. That is where he first meets the Freak, a crippled young boy in braces. Max is impressed with the gutsy Freak who tells everyone he is really a robot. Freak suddenly stops coming to the pre-school and Max does not see him again until third grade when he catches a glimpse of him on the short bus. As the school years pass, Max has more and more problems fitting in with the rest of the kids.

Max overhears his grandparents talk about how worried they are about his sometimes violent behavior. They are even a little afraid of him. They compared him to "Him" which is what they call his father. Max and Freak are reunited when, during the summer before eighth grade, the Freak moves in down the block from Max.

Chapter 2: Up from the Down Under

Max lives in a make-shift room his grandfather made for him in the basement. Even though it is not the greatest, he is glad to be away from the prying eyes of his grandparents. It is summer and his main activity is reading comics. One day he grows tired of his comics and ventures out to the backyard. He is surprised to see that just a few doors down a new family is moving in. The mother, who he later learns is called Fair Gwen, captivates him. To Max, she is as beautiful as a movie star. Max is surprised to see that the Freak is part of the new family. He watches as the Freak bosses all the moving men around, warning them not to damage the box that contains his computer. The Freak has a normal sized head, but his twisted body is not even a yardstick in length. The Fair Gwen tells the Freak, real name Kevin, to go in the backyard and leave the movers alone. Max has secreted himself behind the fence and

some bushes but he is spotted by the Freak who warns him to show
himself or else!

Chapters 1 and 2 Analysis

Chapter 1: The Unvanquished Truth

Both Max and the Freak are misfits in school and in society. Max is not very bright--at least he does not think he is--and has violent tendencies toward other kids and teachers and possibly even his own grandparents who are raising him. His aggressive behavior may stem from the fact that his mother is dead and his estranged father, who apparently has violent behavior similar to his son. The Freak is a crippled young boy in braces but has a spirit that overcomes his disabilities. In fact, the aggressive Max is impressed by the Freak who prefers to call himself a robot instead of a cripple--he has shiny silver braces all the way up his legs. Max tells the reader that he did not have a brain until he merged himself with the Freak which foreshadows a future close relationship between the two boys. The chapter ends with the news that the Freak has just moved down the street from Max. The two will apparently soon connect.

Chapter 2: Up from the Down Under

Although he is not quick to admit it, Max is seeking companionship. He emphasizes that he is not very bright by referring to the fact that his main activity is reading comic books. When he sees the beautiful new neighbor, Fair Gwen, he is taken by her beauty. The obvious question-- is she truly gorgeous or does he just see her that way? Does she fit his ideal of a perfect mother since his own mother is dead? Max is again impressed by the Freak who he sees as bright and strong. Max has more depth than he knows or will admit to--he instantly is able to look past Kevin's twisted body and see a smart and brave young boy.

Chapters 3 and 4 Summary

Chapter 3: American Flyer

Bored in his cellar room again, Max's thoughts keep returning to his new, strange little neighbor. Max ventures out to the backyard again and spots the Freak standing beneath a scraggly tree in his backyard. He is holding his crutch up in the air and making the motion of jumping, although his feet do not leave the ground. The Freak looks angry and gets down on all fours and crawls quickly to a shed. He brings out an old rusted American Flyer wagon and tugs it over to the tree. He manages to climb on the wagon and then reaches with his crutch again but unfortunately still cannot connect with the object he is trying to retrieve from the tree's branches.

Max stealthily approaches but stays his distance--he does not want to be hit by the angry Freak's crutch. Max spots a colorful plastic object in the tree. He pulls the fragile item down and gives it to the Freak. The Freak explains that the object is an ornithopter, or experimental flying bird. For the next hour, the two play with the object. The Freak winds it up and launches it and Max retrieves it. Finally, the rubber band that is providing the propulsion breaks and the game is over. However, Freak tells Max that it just needs some maintenance and it will be operational again.

The Freak is confused when Max mentions his cellar home. Max decides to show instead of tell and pulls the Freak over to his house in his wagon. The Freak looks happy riding along behind Max.

Chapter 4: What Frightened the Fair Gwen

The Freak is impressed with Max's room, especially the fact that he has so much privacy. The Freak explains that he calls his mother "Fair Gwen of Air" after Queen Guinevere from King Arthur. The Freak tells Max the story of King Arthur and how all the strong and brave knights were unable to pull Excalibur, the magical sword from a stone, but the young, weak Arthur was able to pull the sword out and become King.

The Freak is especially impressed with the armor that King Arthur designed for the knights of the Round Table. They were metal-plated and officially the first robots in history he tells Max. King Arthur programmed his "robots," protected by their armor, to go out and slay dragons and monsters. The Freak corrects Max when he says there are not any real robots. He points out how robots are used in assembly lines and machines. The space shuttle even has a robotic arm.

The Freak tells Max that he learns most things by the enormous amount of books he reads. He prefers reading to watching TV--the only show he watches is Star Trek. Max is sure the Freak noticed his serious lacking of books. He fears he will have to admit to being learning disabled but the Freak is so smart he probably figured that out already. The Freak offers to lend him some books. They hear Fair Gwen calling for the Freak who pulls himself up the cellar stairs. Fair Gwen quickly picks him up and runs home with him. Max knows that Fair Gwen is frightened of him.

Chapters 3 and 4 Analysis

Chapter 3: American Flyer

Max already has developed a soft spot in his heart for Freak. He sees that the kid will never be able to get the toy stuck in the tree and Max, without being asked to, gets it for the kid. However, Max has a respectful attitude toward the Freak whose vocabulary is outstanding and intelligence is without question. Despite his physical handicaps, which Max just seems to accept and even in a way forgets, Max admires Freak for who he is and the abilities he has. For his part, the Freak just seems happy that someone has taken an interest in him and is even going to take him home. He probably does not get to go too many places without his mother.

Chapter 4: What Frightened the Fair Gwen

The strength of each character is underscored in this chapter. The Freak is well-read and quite brilliant. He has a love of fantasy--his favorite story is about King Arthur and the Knights of the Round Table. He associates with the young, "wimpy" Arthur who was able to pull the magical sword from the stone--something the big strong knights could not do. His association with this fantasy reveals his dream that he will surpass those with physical strength with his own intelligence and abilities. The Freak refers to the knights as the first robots which has a direct association with Freak's early days in pre-school when he insisted he was a robot. The Freak is making a case for his importance and relevance in society when he emphasizes how many functions are performed by robots.

Max feels inferior to the Freak because he is learning disabled. The Freak knows his intelligence surpasses that of Max's but does not flaunt it. He kindly offers to lend Max some books. When the Freak's mother sees that his tiny son's new companion is the huge, awesome-looking Max, she is frightened. Max is hurt when he realizes that she is afraid of him.

Chapters 5 and 6 Summary

Chapter 5: Spitting Image

Max is under his bed where he can be off on his own cloud somewhere. His grandmother is knocking on the door. Gwen Avery has called her. She wants to apologize for being so rude to Max. She did not realize who he was. She is delighted that the Freak and Max are "making friends." Max's grandmother explains that Gwen and his mother were friends and were pregnant at the same time. Gwen has invited Max for dinner but he is not sure he wants to go. His grandmother encourages him and Max agrees to go.

Gwen is apologetic about her behavior as she busies herself about the kitchen making dinner. Freak is on the floor trying to find pots and pans in the still unpacked boxes. Gwen is talking so fast in trying to make amends to Max that the Freak finally tells her she needs to calm down--she sounds spastic. Gwen finally reveals that Max looks so much like his father who, as it turns out, is in prison. Max is relieved that Gwen no longer seems frightened of him.

Max and the Freak have so much fun together at dinner that Max laughs so hard he chokes on his hot dog. Gwen is very pleased with the budding friendship and expresses how happy she is to be back in the neighborhood. She feels like everyone is getting a fresh start. When Max is back in his cellar, he does not understand why even though he is crying like a baby he feels happy.

Chapter 6: Close Encounter of the Turd Kind

On the way to the Fourth of July celebration by the pond, the Freak and Max encounter Tony D., also known as the Blade, and his gang of punks. Though only seventeen, Tony D. is obviously drunk, and shouts at Max and the Freak, calling them names like Frankenstein and Igor and telling them that they look like a freak show. The Freak puffs himself up and mouths off to Tony D who gives Max a look like he might kill him. Just in the nick of time, the police pass by and Tony D.

and his gang run off. The Freak tells Max he knew he could have taken Tony D. However, when Max explains he would have had to fight the whole gang, the Freak realizes the danger he put them in. They both laugh when the Freak refers to the incident as a "close encounter of the turd kind."

Due to his small stature, the Freak cannot see very well at the fireworks display. Max puts him on his shoulders and the Freak not only enjoys the visual aspect of the fireworks, he shouts out each of the chemical elements that are being used to create the brilliant display.

Chapters 5 and 6 Analysis

Chapter 5: Spitting Image

Gwen is anxious for her son, Kevin, to make friends--probably because he does not have any. Max looks just like his father who, it is revealed, is in prison. Since it was mentioned earlier that Max's father has an anger problem, the reader can speculate that his crime may have been a violent one. It is a heavy burden that the young Max must live with. He looks like his father who is a felon and apparently has a lot of the same behaviors. He has great concern about his future and how much it will parallel his father's life. Another question arises about the death of his mother. Gwen knew his mother when they were young and mentions that his father did not want her to have any friends. Did his anger and jealousy lead him to hurt or maybe kill his mother? Is that why he is in prison? Max and the Freak are off to a good start in their a friendship. Max "cries like a baby" when he returns after dinner with the Freak and Gwen. Max is releasing a lot of built up hurt and anxiety and feels happiness that perhaps he has found a true friend in the Freak.

Chapter 6: Close Encounter of the Turd Kind

The Freak has pride in the strength of his new friend and apparently thinks that Max is capable of defeating any and all enemies. He undoubtedly compares Max to the strong and brave knights of the Round Table while, he, the robot king, is sending his armor-plated knight off to slay the monsters and dragons. The Freak realizes that Max is only human, which is giant step toward a true friendship. By keeping Max as part of his fantasy, the Freak would not be able to appreciate him as a real person who has flaws and weaknesses. The two friends blend their strengths when Max puts the Freak on his shoulders at the fireworks display. The two now make up an awesome entity--a super intelligent brain on a huge and powerful body.

Chapters 7 and 8 Summary

Chapter 7: Walking High Above the World

As Max and the Freak leave the grounds, they head for the lemonade stand nearby. Freak is still on Max's shoulders and spots Tony D. and his gang heading for them. Freak navigates Max away from the approaching punks by digging his left heel or right heel into Max's side, like directing a horse. They are able to escape the gang but Max is uncertain about the Freak's thinking when he heads them right for the pond. Max follows Freak's lead, however, and winds up stuck in the mud in the middle of the pond. Tony D. is short and when he tries to follow them, he is sputtering water. Saved by his gang, Tony D. starts flinging rocks at Max and Freak. The Freak whistles loudly as he sees a squad car approaching. He yells that they need help. The gang runs off and the police assure the boys that they will keep an eye out for the thugs. One of the cops recognizes Max as "Killer Kane's son." However, the Freak tells them that together they are to be known as Freak the Mighty.

Chapter 8: Dinosaur Brain

Max at first fears his grandparents will be upset when he comes home in a cop car soaking wet and full of mud. However, after the police explain what happened, Gram and Grim could not be happier and of course relieved that Max is not in trouble. The cops tell them that Max is a hero, saving the little crippled boy. Funny, Max thinks, that the cops think he saved the Freak when it was the other way around. None the less, he glows in the attention he is getting from his grandparents and the pride that they are obviously feeling for him. Gram even refers to him as "son." Grim thinks it is time for Max to have a cup of coffee-- just like a man. Gram cautions Max to stay away from the thugs. Grim declares that Max can handle them. Somehow strange words come out of Max's mouth, too, like, "Thank you, sir" and "Thanks for the towel, Gram."

Freak interrupts Max's usually lazy summer by banging on his door every morning, announcing what quest they will be going on. Freak explains that the image of slaying dragons simply represents facing the unknown. Max does not quite get Freak's explanation. Freak compares Max's grasp of the situation to the dinosaurs, who had brains the size of peanuts but who none the less ruled the world.

Chapters 7 and 8 Analysis

Chapter 7: Walking High Above the World

Freak is the brains and Max is the brawn in the new being that Freak has dubbed, "Freak the Mighty." The intelligent leadership of Freak is illustrated as he guides Max out of danger. The brawn and strength of Max is showcased when he is able to physically put them out of danger. Each friend makes the other complete. They each recognize their own weaknesses and strengths. It is revealed in this chapter that Max's father is a killer. The question looms, who did he kill?

Chapter 8: Dinosaur Brain

Heroism, just like beauty, is in the eye of the beholder. While the cops and Gram and Grim treat Max like a hero for saving Kevin, Max is surprised that they do not see Kevin as the true hero--he was the brains that led them out of trouble. Gram and Grim have great pride in Max for his actions and in turn Max instantly becomes more respectful towards his grandparents. It is an example of one putting out what one receives. There is much more harmony in the home as the grandparents' fears and suspicions about their huge, possibly violent grandson dissipate and he in turn shows more appreciation of them.

Freak is anxious to face his demons as represented by his fascination with the knights who slay the dragons. Max does not understand Freak's metaphor which underscores Max's inability to think in colors rather than black and white. Freak is trying to widen both their horizons but he needs Max's help to do so.

Chapters 9 and 10 Summary

Chapter 9: Life Is Dangerous

Out on a quest, Freak is in his usual spot atop Max's shoulders. Frank is directing Max through various neighborhoods including a ritzy one which Freak refers to as the Castle of Avarice. Freak claims he is being guided by a compass that was used by Lancelot and even the Black Knight. Even though Freak is very light, after several miles Max is becoming exhausted but Freak pushes him on. They finally come to a large medical research facility. After Max swears on his spit that he will not tell anyone, Freak reveals that he is being fitted for a new body--a fully robotic body. He will be the first person in history to have such a drastic procedure. Freak claims that he has been at the medical center numerous times for fittings for his near body. Max expresses his fear that the procedure would be dangerous to which Freak replies that "life is dangerous."

Chapter 10: Rats or Worse

The next quest that the Freak dreams up takes place in the middle of the night. Just after a tense conversation between Max and Grim about just how smart the Freak really is--Grim not quite believing all the boasting about him by Max--Freak almost makes Max eat his words. Freak tells Max that their next quest is a treasure hunt that is right on their block; the exhausted Max will not have to carry Freak too far. However, the quest must take place exactly at 3:00 am, which is when optimum darkness will occur.

Max and Freak put dirt on their faces and dress in dark clothing so they are not visible in the darkness. Freak is dressed as Darth Vader, minus the mask, and looks comical as he perches atop Max's large shoulders. The target location is the sewer on the corner. Max is unable to pull the grate off the sewer so Freak puts Plan two into effect. Freak pulls out a kite string with a bent paper clip on it and tells Max to lower it down the sewer while he shines a light on the sewer bottom. Max spots the treasure--an old, soggy looking purse. Freak had seen one of Tony D.'s punks hide it in the sewer earlier that day. They open the purse which has no money but they find a credit card in the name of Loretta Lee. Freak declares that she must be a damsel in distress. The next day they will find out that Loretta Lee is a damsel that causes distress.

Chapters 9 and 10 Analysis

Chapter 9: Life Is Dangerous

Freak tells Max to "lift up your hoof" which indicates how strongly Freak is relating to the Knights of the Round Table fantasy. Conveniently, Max does not mind being Freak's horse which enables Freak to live out his fantasy free of conflict. Max is fearful for his new friend who divulges that he will be the first person in history to be fitted with a fully robotic body that will replace his crippled one. The reader is at a crossroads at the conclusion of this chapter. Will the story follow its original roots and remain one of childhood fantasies and friendships or will it take a darker turn towards science fiction or perhaps even tragedy.

Chapter 10: Rats or Worse

Max defends Freak to his grandfather, telling him that Freak knows everything. Max resents Grim referring to Freak as that "poor boy" since Freak is so intelligent and should not be pitied by anyone. Even though Max is portrayed as not very bright, he again surprises by having enough depth to look past the superficial--something his grandparents struggle with. The boys again are playing around some dangerous edges by going after a hidden item stolen by the Tony D. gang. Freak is the one pursuing the thugs which illustrates how naive he is and how much confidence he has that Max can defend him. As smart as he is, foreshadowing suggests that he might be heading toward a lesson in life.

Chapters 11 and 12 Summary

Chapter 11: The Damsel of Distress

The next day, Max and Freak take off for Loretta Lee's residence which, as it turns out, is in the New Tenements, which has come to be known as the New Testaments. Gram has forbidden Max to ever set foot in that neighborhood. However, Freak convinces him that it is okay to disobey if it is for the sake of a quest. They find their way to the tenements which are crumbling and in disarray.

They locate the chain-smoking, harsh Loretta Lee. When she opens the door to find the strange sight of little Freak on top of large Max, she calls to her husband, Iggy, who is inside. Max recognizes Iggy as the leader of a rugged motorcycle gang and both he and Freak become frightened, telling Loretta and Iggy they have the wrong address. Iggy is belittling the two boys, making fun of their size-- referring to them as a circus act. The boys want to leave but Iggy will not let them and insists they come inside.

The boys return the purse to Loretta which compels Iggy to ask about missing cash. Loretta blurts out that there was no cash prompting Iggy to tell her to shut her mouth. Loretta keeps thinking that Max looks familiar and finally remembers that he looks just like Killer Kane. Iggy agrees and says he is the spitting image of his father. Loretta wants them to stay so they can have more "fun" with them but Iggy lets them leave because he does not want Killer Kane to hear that he was hassling his son. Loretta rubs Freak's head, proclaiming that it is good luck to rub a midget's head. Freak does not take her behavior well and tells her he is not a midget and he is not good luck. Loretta gives Freak a parting shot by telling him that his father was a magician because as soon as he heard the phrase "birth defects" he disappeared.

Chapter 12: Killer Kane, Killer Kane, Had a Kid Who Got No Brain

Gram buys Max new clothes and shoes for school. He accompanies her to the mall to buy them--an errand that he hates more than going to the dentist. After their quest to return the purse to Loretta Lee, Freak makes fun of the way the two lowlifes acted. He admits that his father did leave because of his physical condition although his mother refuses to talk about it. Max is relieved that Freak does not bring up his father's past.

Gwen has arranged for Max and Freak to be in the same classes at school so Freak will have an easier time getting around. At first Gram is not in favor of approving the plan because she feels Max should be in the L.D. classes where he will get more help. Finally, she agrees, figuring it cannot hurt for Max to be in the genius class since he has not done that well in the L.D. classes in the past. The first day of school, no one notices the odd pair walking in the halls--with Freak riding on Max's shoulders-- until math class.

There is a new math teacher who calls on Max to tell the class something about his summer. The kids all know that Max never talks in front of class. They start chanting--"Killer Kane had a son with no brain." Freak tells the teacher that he is Kevin sometimes but other times he is Freak the Mighty, killer of dragons and fighter of gangs. He hops atop Max's shoulders and directs him around the room. He repeats Freak the Mighty over and over again until the kids all join in with him. The two wind up in the principal's office for causing a disturbance. Freak is able to convince the principal, using his outstanding vocabulary and powers of persuasion, of the need for their actions.

Chapters 11 and 12 Analysis

Chapter 11: The Damsel of Distress

Freak may well have learned a lesson about going on quests. He finds out that the dragons one meets in real life may not always be easy to slay and might well be impossible to deal with. Even though the boys are trying to help Loretta, the damsel in distress, this low-life and her husband Iggy are not appreciative--they are more interested in making cruel jokes about the appearance of the boys. The reader learns that as tough as Iggy appears to be, he is fearful of Killer Kane, Max's father. Again, there is the question about who Killer Kane killed--was it Max's mother?

It is also revealed that Max has had no contact with his father and has had none since whatever the incident was that put him behind bars. Freak's father apparently abandoned him and his mother after Kevin was born with multiple birth defects. The boys have vast differences-- Max is big and strong and learning disabled while Kevin is small and weak and brilliant. There is one huge factor in common that helps to bond their relationship--their fathers both abandoned them, though for different reasons, at very young ages.

Chapter 12: Killer Kane, Killer Kane, Had a Kid Who Got No Brain

Freak seems more resolved about his missing father than Max does. Freak is able to discuss the fact that his father did abandon him and his mother because of his disabilities. Max, on the other hand, does not want to broach the subject of his own father. In this way, Freak has more strength in facing his past than does Max; however, there is still the question as to the nature of Max's father's crime. Perhaps Max does not know exactly what happened and is afraid to find out--he may not be ready to slay that dragon.

Gram gives a hint of change when she says that since the L.D. classes have not done much for Max that perhaps the genius classes will. Perhaps the school has expected too little of Max and if he is thrown in more advanced classes with Freak he will perform better. Once he is treated like a normal person rather than someone who is not very smart, maybe he will surprise himself and everyone else.

Chapters 13 and 14 Summary

Chapter 13: American Chop Suey

By October of the school year, things are going fairly well. Although Max still will not talk in front of the class, Mrs. Donelli is able to determine that Max is learning and when talking one-on-one with her can provide the correct answers to test questions. He just freezes up in front of the class and is unable to adequately express himself in the written word. The reading skills tutor, Mr. Meehan, is pleased with his progress and Max's test results provide evidence that he is not disabled or dyslexic at all. Mr. Meehan always thought he was just lazy or stubborn or both.

Friday the thirteenth is not a good day for either Max or Freak. Max is called to the office alone where he learns that his father wants him to appear at his parole hearing. Max goes into full panic mode, covering his ears and shouting repeatedly that he does not want to hear about it. The principal, Mrs. Addison, and the school nurse calm him down assuring him that he will not be forced to do anything against his will. Max is so upset that he does not remember how he wound up sitting on the floor with his legs all drawn up. When he sees that the nurse is crying, he fears that he may have hit her during the time he blacked out.

Later in the cafeteria, Freak is eating a second helping of his favorite chop suey when he begins to choke on it. He turns red then purple. In a panic, Max runs for the nurse who tends to him until the ambulance arrives. Even though he recovers to his natural pink color and stops choking, regulations demand that Freak go in the ambulance to the hospital for a thorough check. Mrs. Addison comments that Max has had a rough day which he does not understand because it was Freak, not he, who had the rough day.

Chapter 14: Cross My Heart and Hope to Die

The Freak comes home from the hospital and he is fine. Gwen orders him to stay in bed for a few days but allows Max to visit him. Freak shushes Max when he brings up his robotic body replacement, revealing that Gwen is against it. Everything stays on an even keel until Christmas. Max is downstairs when he hears his grandparents arguing-- something that never happens. He sneaks up and overhears that Grim wants to get his gun to protect his family and Gram is crying that "He" will come in and take it from Grim and shoot him. Grim reminds Gram that "he" cannot be trusted and how Annie found that out the hard way. Grim tries to comfort her because she is so upset and worried. Max knows exactly who they are talking about.

Later, Grim comes down and discusses the matter with Max who is on Grim's side about getting a gun. Grim usually does not seem old but on this day, he seems about a thousand years old. Grim says if he does get a gun, he will have to lie to Gram about it. Max promises he will not tell Gram. Grim tells Max that his father might get out on parole and that he went to the court and got a restraining order prohibiting his father from coming in within a mile of their house. Just to be on the safe side, Grim makes Max promise that he will stay inside the house for the next few days.

Chapters 13 and 14 Analysis

Chapter 13: American Chop Suey

Max is smarter than anyone has given him credit for. He is in the advanced classes and is keeping up although he is unable to express his answers in writing or in front of a class. It is confirmed by the reading specialist that he has no disability; his problems in school may prove to be more closely associated with emotional problems. Max adamantly refuses to discuss his father or hear anything about him. He reacts with a combination of anger and fear when his father's name is mentioned. Those emotions have certainly played havoc with his young mind and been responsible for at least some of his learning problems.

Max does not realize that his emotional problems are on a par with Freak's physical problems. He has not developed enough self-worth and maturity to realize that emotional distress can be just as debilitating as physical ones. Another question arises: was Freak's choking spell just a random incident or is there some other physical problem that is looming?

Chapter 14: Cross My Heart and Hope to Die

Max's avoidance of his father may be over. A confrontation may soon be a reality if his father gets out on parole. When Grim reminds Gram that it backfired on Annie when she trusted Ken, it brings up the question again as to just what happened between them. We know from this conversation and their fear of Max's father that there was probably a violent incident. Max is totally on his grandfather's side against his father, once again illustrating his fear and anger toward his father. Gram is upset and crying over the situation, which is made worse during Christmas when memories of her deceased daughter are surely already engulfing her.

Chapters 15 and 16 Summary

Chapter 15: What Came Down the Chimney

Freak and Fair Gwen come to Max's house for Christmas Eve dinner. Everyone stuffs themselves--Gwen watches Freak so he does not eat too fast. Grim tells some funny stories about when he was a kid. He claims that his family was so poor that he did not get a lump of coal in his stocking--his father would have to write the word "coal" on a piece of paper and put it in his stocking because they could not afford the real thing. After dinner there are lots of presents. Max gives Freak a gizmo that has all kinds of tools on it. He figures that Freak will be able to invent something with it. Freak's gift to Max is contained in a pyramid-shaped box that Freak constructed himself. When Max follows the instructions and pushes on a certain spot, the whole box opens automatically, prompting Grim to finally admit that Freak is a genius. Freak created a dictionary of his favorite words as his gift to Max.

Later that night, a cold draft wakes Max up in his cellar room. He thinks it is odd because the room is always so warm. Suddenly, a large hand is over his mouth and a voice tells him not to say a word.

Chapter 16: A Chip Off the Old Block

Max's father makes him get dressed. Max feels numb, almost like he is in a dream, a dream he had always feared would come true. He goes through the motions and answers his father's questions as politely as possible. They leave the cellar and head out in the snow. Although he knows it is freezing out, somehow Max does not feel it even without a coat. Ken gets Max in the streetlight to get a good look at him. He is pleased that Max looks just like him--that he is a chip off the old block. When Max makes a comment that is not in answer to a question from his father, Ken warns him not to sass him. He also tells Max that his grandparents have poisoned his mind against him and that he never killed anyone.

They head out for the tenements and arrive at Loretta and Iggy's apartment. It is obvious that they are expected from the greeting Ken and Max get. Loretta is a little tipsy which disturbs Ken who told them there would be no drinking. Loretta sarcastically refers to Ken as Preacher Kane. Even though it is the middle of the night, Iggy makes the two of them greasy hamburgers, which Max can hardly get down his throat. Iggy tells Ken that he'll show him the apartment he told him about.

Chapters 15 and 16 Analysis

Chapter 15: What Came Down the Chimney

The friendship of Max and Freak is uniting their two families. After a
pleasant Christmas Eve, Max is finally going to be forced to face his
past by the presence of his father. Did his father escape from prison or
was he paroled? Does he plan to take Max with him? If he was granted
a parole, he has already violated it by ignoring the restraining order
Grim obtained against him.

Chapter 16: A Chip Off the Old Block

Max is kidnapped by his father. He is so frightened that he is numb, in
shock--he is living the nightmare scenario that he has feared for a long
time. His father is abrupt with him and though he tells Max that he
never killed anyone and that Max's mind has been poisoned against
him, Max does not feel any better. Loretta and Iggy are aiding and
abetting Ken who is either a parolee or escapee and the kidnapper of
Max. Loretta's comment about Preacher Kane is either a red herring or
an indication that maybe Ken tried to change his ways. Iggy apparently
has arranged for a place for Ken and Max to stay.

Chapters 17 and 18 Summary

Chapter 17: By All That's Holy

The place that Iggy takes Ken and Max to is an old lady's apartment. Iggy, knowing that the old lady is out of town, broke into it. It will be a temporary place for them to stay. Ken warns Max not to try to run away. To make sure he does not, Ken ties Max's hands and feet in a rope that is linked to Ken's waist. Ken is exhausted and sleeps for a short while on the floor next to Max's chair. When he awakes, he tells Max that they need to have a man to man talk. He picks up the old lady's Bible and swears on it that he never killed Max's mother. He tells Max that a great injustice was done to him and that he suffered for years locked up for something he did not do. He asks Max if he got the presents and letters he sent. Max responds that he did not, which does not surprise Ken. In the dim light, Max can see tears streaming down Ken's face. After their talk, Ken lays back down on the floor by Max's chair and falls asleep. Max cannot sleep and struggles hard not to think about things he does not want to remember.

Chapter 18: Never Trust a Cripple

Loretta brings leftover pizza to Ken and Max but Ken does not want it. He tells Loretta to send Iggy over. They hunt for food in the old lady's kitchen but only come up with cornflakes that Max eats with water. Ken tells Max that they will be moving to a warmer climate and that they will be getting a large bus to travel in. On the side of the bus will be a big sign that says "The Reverend Kenneth David Kane." Max will help collect money from people wanting to hear the Reverend Ken preach. Ken ties up Max again, telling him that he has to keep him tied until he sees the light and realizes that he, Ken, is the light.

Ken panics when he sees the blue lights of an approaching police car. When Iggy comes, Ken accuses him of turning him in. Iggy denies it saying that the little crippled boy was in the police car and that he is the one that led the cops to the tenements. Iggy tells Ken that the crippled boy is a friend of Max. Ken warns Max to never trust a cripple.

Chapters 17 and 18 Analysis

Chapter 17: By All That's Holy

Ken claims to have been unjustly convicted of the murder of Max's mother. He accuses Grim and Gram of keeping his presents and letters from him, although they do not seem to be those kind of people. Ken is trying to poison Max's mind against the people who have raised him most of his life. The tears streaming down Ken's face either indicate his pain over being accused of a horrible crime he did not commit or tears of guilt over a horrible crime that he did commit.

Chapter 18: Never Trust a Cripple

Ken plans to use Max to collect money in the preacher scam he is planning. Max must feel some hope of escape when he hears that Freak is guiding the police in their direction. If there was a glimmer of hope in Max's mind that his father is really a good man, it now evaporates. His father is abusing him and plans on using him in an illegal operation.

Chapters 19 and 20 Summary

Chapter 19: Into the Black Down Under

Ken takes Max next door to a boarded up abandoned unit. Ken orders Max to descend the stairs to the dark, damp basement, which is difficult because he is still tied up. He stumbles a few times but finally makes it down the steps. Ken sticks a rag in Max's mouth and tells him he has to go see Iggy about the car he is getting for them.

Loretta comes down the stairs with her flashlight. As she tries to free him, Loretta tells Max that the plan is for Iggy to keep Ken busy while she unties Max. With all the cops crawling around outside, she is sure they will be safe. She has trouble untying the ropes and finds a jagged piece of metal to cut through the rope . She finally frees him. He stands up and is a little unsteady on his feet. Max sees two large hands coming out of the dark and closing around Loretta's neck. Ken is strangling Loretta.

Chapter 20: Freak the Mighty Strikes Again

Max can see that Loretta is fading fast. He wants to intervene but he can hardly walk. He falls on top of Ken and yells to stop because he is killing her. He screams at his father telling him that he saw him kill his mother and that he has never forgotten. He strangled his mother just like he is trying to strangle Loretta. Finally, Ken lets go of Loretta who is barely breathing and focuses on Max. Ken tells Max that it is impossible for him to remember when his mother died because he was only four years old. Max tells his father that after he had locked him in his room, he broke the window and yelled for help. The police responded and rushed to the scene, arresting Ken that very night. Ken realizes that it was Max who alerted the police all those years ago and now blames Max for his arrest. He starts to squeeze Max's neck who is too weak to fight him off. Next thing he knows, the small basement window is broken and Freak is standing there with a water gun.

Ken figures that Freak is no threat but Freak tells him that his gun is filled with sulfuric acid. Freak shoots a stream of liquid from his water gun right in Ken's eyes. Max grabs Freak down from the window ledge and heads for the stairs. Ken is screaming and rubbing his eyes but is right behind the boys, grabbing at them. Max eludes him and finally reaches the first floor where a plywood barrier is between them and the outdoors. He protects Freak's little body and crashes through the wood. He is greeted by a red-eyed Iggy and dozens of cops. Iggy is relieved to see that Loretta is still alive after she is brought out by some of the cops. Freak actually used vinegar, curry powder and soap in his water gun but the sting makes Ken think he was blinded. Ken is cuffed and taken away by the police. Gram and Grim and Gwen run up to the boys, relieved that they are both safe.

Chapters 19 and 20 Analysis

Chapter 19: Into the Black Down Under

Loretta has a heart after all and tries to free Max. Iggy is in on the plan
as well, probably figuring the cops are about to catch up with Ken and
he does not want to appear complicit in a kidnapping. Unfortunately,
Ken catches her and while it may not have been her first good deed, it
may be her last. Does Loretta die? How will Ken react? Will he think
that Max was in on the escape plan and make him the next victim?

Chapter 20: Freak the Mighty Strikes Again

When Ken is strangling Loretta, the memories of Max's father killing
his mother all rush back to him. He remembers the incident during the
intervening years, which causes him great emotional stress. Perhaps it
causes his inability to express himself, afraid of what he might blurt
out. The scene with Ken strangling Loretta is reminiscent of his
mother's death right down to the broken window. It is not clear if the
memory of his mother's murder is a conscious memory or it if all
comes out with the attempted murder of Loretta. A broken window and
the police save Max the first time but this time it is a broken window
and Freak who saves the day. Freak cleverly fools Ken into thinking he
is blinded by the "sulfuric acid" that he says is in the water gun. The
little crippled boy brings down Killer Kane--Freak and Max will surely
be hailed as heroes.

Chapters 21 and 22 Summary

Chapter 21: The Accident of Nature

Max is checked out at the hospital and spends many hours at the police station telling the cops what happened. Loretta has a cracked bone in her neck but she will be okay. Iggy is worried to death about her. Max thinks that Iggy is a much better person that he thought he was. Gram insists that Max sleep upstairs for the time being--which is actually fine with Max. Gwen really gets after Freak about risking his life. She tells him his quests are over. She is worried about his breathing--his insides are growing but his outside is not. He is spending more time at the medical center. Fair Gwen still does not know the details of the robotic body transplant.

Mrs. Donelli posts a picture from the newspaper of Freak and Max on the bulletin board. The very first day somebody draws mustaches on them. Freak thinks he looks good in a mustache and cannot wait until he can grow a real one. The police want Max to testify at the trial of his father. He is not looking forward to it but he will do whatever it takes to make sure Ken stays in jail the rest of his life. Good news comes when Grim is informed that Ken has struck a plea deal and will serve out his present term plus ten years, which would make him a very old man if he ever gets out.

Grim tells Max that he is like his father in looks and size but that is where it ends. What is important is that he has his mother's heart. Max is worried how he will turn out when he grows up.

Chapter 22: Remembering Is Just an Invention of the Mind

School is out and Freak the Mighty is one year old. A short time after school is let out, it is Freak's thirteenth birthday. Gwen has Max, Grim and Gram over for dinner and cake. Freak keeps spouting off that he wants a ride on the space shuttle or a Learjet for his birthday. Max knows that Freak is getting the computer he has been drooling over and that he will be thrilled. Freak does not eat much at dinner but Max figures he is saving room for a big piece of cake. Freak asks Max to blow out the candles while he makes a wish. Freak does not eat his cake either. Gram and Max are helping Gwen clean up in the kitchen. Suddenly they hear a commotion in the other room. Everyone rushes in to find Kevin wheezing with his eyes rolled back in their sockets. Kevin is having a seizure; Gwen calls 911. Max rushes outside to wave the ambulance in.

Chapters 21 and 22 Analysis

Chapter 21: The Accident of Nature

Max is willing to do his part to make sure his father is put away the rest of his life. The boy who could not bring himself to talk in front of a classroom has certainly grown, not out of desire but out of necessity. He is now willing to speak in front of judge, jury, lawyers, the courtroom, the press and his own father to tell the world how his father tried to kill Loretta.

Freak's insides are growing but his outside is not. His lungs, heart and all his other organs are in danger--they are being crowded inside his body. He mentions that he is going to the medical center more often. As his condition worsens, he still holds on to his fantasy of getting a new robotic body. Max does not seem to doubt Freak and will be totally unprepared if the worse should happen to Freak.

Chapter 22: Remembering Is Just an Invention of the Mind

Freak is more ill than Max has realized. He asks Max to blow out his candles because he does not have enough wind to do so himself. Freak is trying to hide his fears by talking about wanting a ride on the space shuttle or on a Learjet. Max is worried. They have been inseparable for a year. The ambulance cannot get there soon enough for Max.

Chapters 23, 24 and 25 Summary

Chapter 23: The Empty Book

Kevin is in the ICU with no visitors allowed other than his mother. Max decides to walk over there anyway just on the chance he will get to see Freak. He runs into Gwen who is all teary-eyed. She hugs him and tells him that Freak is insisting on seeing him. Dr. Spivak tells Max he can only stay a short while and not to touch anything. Max is surprised at how tiny Freak looks on the big hospital bed with tubes seemingly everywhere. Freak shows Max the tracheotomy procedure he has to have in order to breathe. He thinks it is cool and sticks his finger on the tracheotomy button whistling the theme for Star Trek through the opening in his throat.

Max asks when Freak can come home. Kevin says he will not be coming home in his present body and that the robotic surgery team is on alert. It will be awhile before he will be fully operational because he will have to learn to walk on his new tall legs. Kevin tells Max to pick up the book on his nightstand. When Max opens it, he finds only blank pages. Kevin tells Max to write down the details, the laughs, the ups and downs of every one of their quests. Max reminds Kevin that he is not able to write his thoughts down but Kevin insists he must because he, Kevin, will not be able to--he will be tied up for quite a while. Kevin has a choking spell from which he recovers but the doctor has Max leave.

At dinner Grim says how sad he feel for poor Gwen. Max reminds him that it is Freak who's going through the operation not Gwen. Max's grandparents look stunned but remain silent.

Chapter 24: The Return Kicker

Max leaves home early thinking he might be able to sneak in and see Kevin. When he gets to the ICU, he notices that all the nurses look like they are crying. He hears one of them say to get Dr. Spivak because she was Kevin's doctor. It dawns on Max then that his friend has died. He goes berserk and runs down the hall, kicking and screaming. He punches his fist through the glass door of the Medical Research facility that has a sign that says "No Admittance." The hospital police and Dr. Spivak catch up with him. She takes responsibility for him. While she bandages his hand, she listens to him rave at her about her lying to Kevin about getting a robotic body. Dr. Spivak explains that Kevin used fantasy in order to cope with his condition. He had known from the age of seven that he would not live very long. Kevin died because his heart got to big for his body.

Chapter 25: What Loretta Said

Max hides in his basement for days and days and misses Kevin's funeral and Gwen's departure. She cannot stand to live in the house without Kevin there. Max is not happy about going to school the next fall but Grim warns him he will drag him there if he has to. He hates the way everyone feels sorry for him--even Tony D. However, he and Tony are enemies again--just the way Max likes it--because Max tells him if he ever feels sorry for him again he will pound him down headfirst in the millpond. Max runs into Loretta who tells him that Gwen moved to California and has a new boyfriend. Loretta asks him what he is doing and when he responds "nothing," Loretta says, "Nothing is a drag, kid. Think about it" (160). Somehow Loretta's words inspire him. Max goes home and picks up the empty book Kevin gave him and he starts writing and writing and writing. He writes during the whole semester and winds up writing a whole book. He is thinking about reading some too.

Chapters 23, 24 and 25 Analysis

Chapter 23: The Empty Book

Kevin's condition worsens. He tells Max that he will not be coming home in his current state. Once he gets his new robotic body, it will take him a while to get used to it. Max is still unaware at the grave situation his friend is in and his naivete is allowing him to believe Kevin's story about a robotic body transplant. Gwen, Grim and Gram do not seem to be aware that Max is totally in the dark about his best friend. They are caught up in their own worries and concerns so much so that they do not realize how vulnerable Max is to a serious emotional set back if Kevin does not make it.

Kevin is trying to help his friend by encouraging him to write--writing is one of the skills that Max's emotional trauma took from him. Kevin will not take no for an answer--he insists that it must be Max who writes the stories of the adventures that they shared over the last year.

Chapter 24: The Return Kicker

Although Max temporarily returns to his violent ways after learning of Kevin's death, he is able to calm down when Dr. Spivak, in a very kindly way, explains Kevin's condition and what caused him to die. She does not treat Max like a child or like a learning disabled person, she treats him like an intelligent adult. Max realizes that Kevin lived in a fantasy world because the real world had too many dragons for him to slay.

Chapter 25: What Loretta Said

In his grief, Max isolates himself--physically and emotionally. However, his grandparents refuse to give up on him and insist that he come out of the room and return to school. Max learns that you never know who might inspire you; it could be a chain-smoking alcoholic who tells you you're wasting your life, or a little crippled boy who just might motivate you to write a book.

Characters

Maxwell Kane

Max is about fourteen years old when he writes about the quests and adventures he and his best friend, Freak, undertook over their year together as "Freak the Mighty." Max is a really big kid. He is tall and stocky and very strong for his age. He has earned a reputation as being a little on the rough, even violent, side. His grandparents fear that he might become violent like his father, who is known as Killer Kane. Max does not do well in school even though he gets help in the learning disabled class and he does not have any friends--that is, until he meets up with Kevin, the Freak, who moves in a few doors down from his house.

Kevin is a crippled little boy but the smartest person Max has ever met. They become best friends and when Killer Kane gets out on parole and kidnaps his son, it is the Freak who comes to the rescue. When Killer Kane almost kills Loretta, a woman who is trying to free him from his father's grasp, the scene comes back to him when he witnessed his father killing his mother many years before. The emotional trauma has made Max angry and even violent at times and is responsible for his poor performance in school. After his father is returned to jail, Max realizes what is important in his life--his loving grandparents and his friends, especially the Freak.

Kevin Avery [Freak]

Kevin Avery, also known as Freak, is a twelve-year old boy whose normal-sized head resides over a twisted body that is less than a yard in length. He is born with multiple birth defects and over the years his condition progressively worsens because his organs are growing while his body remains the same size. Freak is brilliant though. His best friend, Max, considers Freak the smartest person he has ever met--a sheer genius. Kevin knows something about everything. He reads books on every subject imaginable. His vocabulary is so advanced that Max often does not know what he is talking about.

However, Kevin has a healthy and vivid imagination. He identifies with King Arthur and the Knights of the Round Table. He feels a connection with King Arthur who, as a young, weak boy, is able to pull the magical sword Excalibur out of its stone when the brave and powerful knights cannot. Kevin feels an allegiance to the knights as well; in Kevin's mind, his silver leg braces match their suits of armor. When Kevin and Max become best friends, Kevin and his imagination lead the lethargic, unimaginative Max on quests and adventures, slaying monsters and dragons all the way.

By a sequence of events, Kevin is able to save his friend's life. There is one dragon he cannot slay, however. Though their friendship lasts only one year, the memory of Max's best friend lives on to inspire Max to believe in himself.

Gram

Gram is Max's grandmother. Gram and her husband are raising Max. Gram is always worried about Max's welfare. She is a doting grandmother who gets on Max's nerves but she is always on his side and there to support him.

Grim

Grim is Max's grandfather. Grim and his wife are raising Max. Although Max often thinks his grandfather is a pain, Grim loves his grandson and protects him. He wants only the best for Max.

Gwen the Fair

Max is enamored when his beautiful new neighbor, Gwen, moves in. She is Freak's mother. Freak dubs his lovely mother Gwen the Fair because she reminds him of Guinevere of Camelot.

Killer Kane

Killer Ken Kane is Max's father. Killer Kane is in jail for murdering Max's mother. When he gets out on parole, he kidnaps Max. The police eventually catch up with him and return him to jail.

Annie

Annie is Grim and Gram's daughter. She is strangled to death by Killer Kane when Max is only four years old. Max witnesses the killing of his mother, which naturally traumatizes him.

Loretta

Loretta is a chain-smoking, alcoholic friend of Killer Kane. Although she at first is helping Killer Kane in the kidnapping of Max, she has a change of heart and frees Max, which almost costs her her life.

Iggy

Iggy is Loretta's husband. He is helping Killer Kane after he is paroled from prison. He eventually helps the police catch Killer and is greatly relieved that Loretta is still alive.

Tony D.

Tony D. is the leader of a gang of punks who ridicule Max and Freak, calling them a circus act. The police come on the scene when Tony D. and his gang are about to brutalize Max and Freak.

Objects/Places

Pre-School

Max and Kevin, the Freak, first meet when they attend the same pre-school.

Max's House

Max lives with his grandfather and grandmother in their house. Max's grandfather has made a room for Max in the cellar. Kevin and his mother come to Max's house for Christmas Eve.

Kevin's House

Kevin lives with his mother in a house a few doors down from Max's house. Max and his grandparents come for dinner and cake at Kevin's house for the Freak's thirteenth birthday.

The Tenements

Max and Freak return Loretta's purse to her, which is stolen by Tony D. and his gang. Killer Kane brings Max over to the tenements after he kidnaps him.

The Medical Research Facility

Freak tells Max that he is going to be the first human in history to have a full body transplant; he will be receiving a fully robotic body in a risky operation at the Medical Research building.

ICU

When Kevin becomes progressively worse, he is taken to the ICU at the local hospital. Kevin dies in the ICU and Max loses control when he realizes he has lost his best friend.

School - Eighth Grade

Max is in the learning disabled classes until Gwen asks that Max be allowed to attend the advanced classes with Freak so he can help him get around. Max does better in the gifted class than he does in the learning disabled classes.

The Millpond

The millpond is where the 4th of July celebration is held. Later that night, Tony D. and his gang chase Max and Freak into the middle of the pond but they are rescued when the police run the punks off.

Fourth of July Celebration

When Kevin cannot see the fireworks because of his short stature, Max swings him up on his broad shoulders; this is the night that "Freak the Mighty" was born.

The Black Cellar

Killer Kane, Max's father, ties him up in a dark basement of an abandoned apartment. Max is almost strangled by his father but Freak is able to save him.

Themes

The Soft Bigotry of Low Expectations

There are many examples in "Freak the Mighty" in which others expect less of Max--and then are surprised when that is what they get. Max never thinks he is very bright; but looking more closely, he is told--told officially--that he is not very smart. Since Max cannot talk in front of his classes and cannot adequately write down test answers on his paper, he is immediately labeled as learning disabled.

The fact that his mother is dead, murdered by his father, does not enter the minds of these experts as a possible reason for his poor performance in school. The trauma of a four-year-old witnessing the murder of his mother at the hands of his father would surely provide the reason for his isolation and lack of self-worth. As a result, Max does not do well in school, even with special help. This only serves to confirm the low opinion he already has of himself.

Many people fear the twelve-year-old. After all, his father is Killer Kane and Max is big and stocky just like his father. Even his own grandparents fear he will be like "him" when he grows up. It is no wonder that Max acts out at certain times, displaying anger and even violence. It is expected of him and he obliges.

Max draws strength from his friend, Kevin, who believs in him and does not focus on any perceived flaws. When Max is assigned to attend Kevin's classes--which are for gifted kids--so he can help Kevin get around, surprisingly Max does better than he did when he was getting special help. He keeps up and is finally declared free of learning disabilities. When he is expected to keep up in the gifted class, he does just that.

Seeing The Best in People

Max is the narrator of the story and often comments about how bright his friend the Freak is. He never has conditional praise for his friend, qualifying Kevin's abilities with comments like "Freak is smart for a crippled boy," or "at least he's smart." In fact, Max becomes irritated if anyone refers to Freak as "poor Kevin." Max thinks to himself, "poor Kevin?" wondering how anyone could look at Kevin with pity. After all, he is a genius, reading everything he can get his hands on and knowing something on every subject that comes up. Max, who does not consider himself a great thinker at all, has a lot more depth than he gives himself credit for. He is able to look past the exterior of a person and see his strengths, almost not noticing any flaws.

There are many examples of Max's ability to find the substance in his friend. When they first meet in pre-school, Max takes notice of the little crippled boy wearing braces and proclaiming loudly that he is a robot. When Kevin and his mother move into the neighborhood, Max is in awe of the tiny 12-year-old barking orders at the movers, cautioning them not to damage the box with his computer. When Max observes Kevin's futile attempt to retrieve a toy helicopter stuck in a tree, he does not belittle him or pity him. Rather, he admires his ingenuity in crawling on hands and knees and dragging a wagon back with him to stand on. When others ridicule Kevin's physical condition, Max cannot understand why their focus is on his body instead of his mind. Even though Max is big and strong in body, he never feels less than lucky to be Freak's friend.

True Friendship

Max and Kevin develop a true friendship--they accept each others' flaws and praise each others abilities. While Max and Freak are very different, there are many ways in which they are alike. They draw courage from each others' strengths. For what Kevin, the Freak, lacks in strength, he defers to Max who has the brawn and size. The intelligence that Max thinks he does not have is completed by Freak's bright and imaginative brain.

The author creates a metaphor of friendship as a true oneness, a real union of two bodies and two souls. The image of the tiny, fragile body of the disabled Kevin riding atop the strong, wide shoulders of Max represents the entity that they feel they had become--Freak the Mighty. Max even comments that with Kevin riding on his shoulders, he finally has a brain up there. Kevin is living his fantasy as well, finally having "tall legs." They complete each other.

When Kevin succumbs to his disabilities--his organs are crowded in a body that refuses to grow-- understandably Max initially feels lost--part of him dies. However, Kevin's spirit and inspiration do not die with his weak, twisted body. Instead, he leaves these qualities as a priceless legacy to his best friend Max. In turn, Max fulfills Kevin's last wish and writes the story of their adventures and their friendship, something he never would have thought he could do.

Style

Point of View

The story is told in first-person narrative, with Max as the narrator. Max begins his story by describing the first time he and his friend, Kevin, also known as Freak, meet. They are toddlers in pre-school. Kevin stands out in Max's memory because the fragile little boy has such a twisted body and is wearing leg braces and proclaims that he is a robot.

Max tells the story of the unusual and close relationship that the two boys eventually develop when Kevin moves in a few doors down from Max's house the summer before both begin eighth grade. Max relates all his self-doubts about his intelligence and abilities and his astonishment at how bright Kevin is. Although Freak does not have much of a body, his brain more than makes up for it. Although Max is labeled as learning disabled because he cannot talk in front of the class or answer test questions in writing, it later emerges that his inability to communicate is actually the result of a traumatic event that occurred in his young childhood.

Max tells of his fear of turning out like his father, who his grandparents can only refer to as "he." As the story proceeds, the reader learns that Max's mother is dead and that his father may have killed her. Finally, when Max's memories rush out when he is threatened by his father, it is then that Max reveals that he witnessed the murder of his mother by his father.

When the progressively declining Kevin succumbs to his disabilities, he tells Max that he must be the one to write the story of their adventures and their friendship. Max does not think he has the ability to write such a work but the memory of Kevin inspires him. As the book ends, the reader learns that Max writes the book at Kevin's suggestion.

Setting

The story of "Freak the Mighty" takes place in an unnamed town that is probably located in the mid-west or northeast since there is mention of snow storms. Max lives in a house with his grandparents who are raising him. Kevin and his mother Gwen move into a house a few doors down from Max's house. Gwen is a single mother and Kevin is disabled. The neighborhood is apparently modest since Gwen probably could not afford an upscale neighborhood.

Max lives in a make-shift room that his grandfather made for him in the cellar. Although it is not the most attractive room, Max loves it because he can get away from his grandparents and have some privacy. Max and Freak attend a Fourth of July celebration at the millpond. It is there that Max hoists the small and fragile Freak on his shoulders so he can see the fireworks display and when "Freak the Mighty" is born--Kevin's brilliant mind atop Max's strong, large body.

An apartment complex called the Tenements plays a role in the story. It is where Loretta and Iggy live and where Killer Kane takes his son, Max, after he kidnaps him from his grandparents' home. A large medical research facility and hospital is where the ailing Kevin is taken before his death.

Language and Meaning

"Freak the Mighty" is written in a clever manner that captures the language of young teenagers but strikes a balance that is appealing to children and adults alike. It is an intelligent account of the friendship of two boys who at first blush have little in common but in the end developed a close relationship in which each boy completes the other. Kevin, also known as the Freak, is a crippled young boy with a normal sized head and a fragile twisted body. Max is a tall, stocky young man who is much bigger than the other kids.

Kevin reads everything he can get his hands on. His vocabulary is advanced and his imagination is healthy and, unlike his body, knows no bounds. Max, who has been wrongly labeled as learning disabled, is impressed and amazed by Kevin's vocabulary--he often has to ask him to explain what he is talking about in simpler language. With the tiny Kevin atop Max's strong, broad shoulders they together form "Freak the Mighty." Kevin is the brains while Max is the vehicle they take on their quests to slay dragons and defeat monsters. Kevin's rich vocabulary and creative descriptions are contained in a lexicon that follows the main story. It is filled with his imaginative descriptions and his obvious sense of fun.

Structure

"Freak the Mighty" is divided into twenty-five chapters. The story is followed by Freak's dictionary, which is the lexicon of his favorite words with descriptions from the vivid imagination of young Kevin, or Freak, as he is affectionately dubbed by Max. The story is told by Max who looks back on his year with his best friend, Freak, and how together they form Freak the Mighty.

The story of Max and Freak's friendship progresses in a straightforward manner and in a largely chronological fashion. The tale begins with Max's memories of the two of them together at a pre-school after which they do not reunite again until the summer before eighth grade. Max describes how a young boy with a seemingly angry and violent nature is tempered through his friendship with the brilliant though very ill Kevin.

Max describes the struggles of each boy, their differences and their similarities. Although for different reasons, neither boy has any friends. Max is not very bright or does not think he is, but is big and strong. Kevin is the brains of the duo, but his body is fragile and twisted from multiple birth defects. When Kevin knows he will not live much longer, he insists that Max write the story of their friendship, which takes the reader back to where the book begins.

Quotes

"I invented games like kick-boxing and kick-knees and kick-faces and kick-teachers and kick-the-other -little-day-care-critters, because I knew what a rotten lie that hug stuff was." (Chapter 1, p. 2)

"This time I don't say huh because then I might have to explain how I'm an L.D., and reading books is the last thing I want to do, right after trimming my toenails with a lawn mower, gargling nails, and eating worms for breakfast." (Chapter 4, p. 19)

"'He's not a poor boy,' I say. 'You should hear him talk. I think the rest of him is so small because his brain is so big.'" (Chapter 5, p. 24)

"Freak is making a fuss because he can't see. There are so many people crowded around, all he can see are feet and knees, and people are lifting their little kids up to see the fireworks explode like hot pink flowers in the sky, and so I just sort of reach down without thinking and pick up Freak and set him on my shoulders." (Chapter 6, p. 34)

"Shh! Speak of this to no one, but at some future time as yet undetermined, I will enter that lab and become the first bionically improved human." (Chapter 9, p. 51)

"Freak is riding up top, which he almost always does now. That way he doesn't have to wear his leg brace or carry his crutches, and besides, I like how it feels to have a really smart brain on my shoulders, helping me think." (Chapter 11, p. 64)

"Hey, midget man? I know all about you. Your old man was a magician, did you know that?...He must be a magician, because as soon as he heard the magic words 'birth defect,' he disappeared." (Chapter 11, p. 71)

"Christmas Eve is real quiet. Like Freak says, 'You could hear a mouse fart.' Which, even if it is a stupid joke, makes Grim smile and shake his head." (Chapter 15, p. 93)

"The Gram opens her present from me, which is a bracelet made of shells from beaches around the world, and she right away puts it on and says it's just what she wanted. Which is so like Gram--if you gave her an old beer can she'd act pleased and say it was just what she wanted." (Chapter 15, p. 95)

"I'm in this faraway place, falling backwards real slow and dreamy, when I hear a window breaking. Then a small faraway voice is saying, 'Put your hands up, villain!' and I really am falling and the air is coming back into my lungs so fast, it hurts." (Chapter 20, p. 131)

"'The man is an accident of nature,' he says. 'all you got from him is your looks and your size. You've got your mother's heart, and that's what counts.'" (Chapter 21, p. 139)

"I don't know if this makes sense, but for a long time I felt like I was a balloon and somebody had let the air out of me. I didn't care if I ever got the air back, because what does it really matter if we're all going to die in the end?" (Chapter 25, p. 158)

Topics for Discussion

How does Kevin, the Freak, use fantasy to cope with his condition? How does he relate to King Arthur? To the Knights of the Round Table?

What causes people to think that Max might be dangerous? What happened to Max's mother?

What similarities do Max and Kevin have? How are they different? How does one friend complete the other?

What does Max learn from Kevin? What does he learn from Loretta? Who does Max have support from although he does not always realize it?

How does Ken, Max's father, plan to use him? After Ken is paroled from prison, does he have a religious conversion or have his criminal ways remain unchanged? What crimes does he commit after leaving prison?

Why is it difficult for Max to talk in front of the class? What could have caused Max's difficulty in communicating? What assessment does Max receive from the reading tutor?

Even though they are good friends, what important things does Max and Kevin not understand about each other? What opinions do they have of each other? How are they mistaken and how are they correct?

CPSIA information can be obtained
at www.ICGtesting.com
Printed in the USA
LVOW11s0846190418
574088LV00001B/123/P